# Beside the Muezzin's Call
# &
# Beyond the Harem's Veil

*poems by*

# Saba Syed Razvi

*Finishing Line Press*
Georgetown, Kentucky

# Beside the Muezzin's Call
# &
# Beyond the Harem's Veil

*This book is dedicated to my mother, who taught
me with love that faith and dreams transcend
the oppression of fear.*

Copyright © 2017 by Saba Syed Razvi
ISBN 978-1-63534-060-0   First Edition
All rights reserved under International and Pan-American Copyright Conventions.
No part of this book may be reproduced in any manner whatsoever without written permission from the publisher, except in the case of brief quotations embodied in critical articles and reviews.

ACKNOWLEDGMENTS

I'd like to thank the publications that featured earlier or other versions of some of these poems: *Voices of Resistance: Muslim Women on War, Faith, & Sexuality*, edited by Sarah Husain; *Of the Divining and the Dead*, a chapbook, published by Finishing Line Press; *Project Peace: an Anthology*, edited by Melissa Studdard; *Tahzeeb-e-Deccan*, a magazine, edited by Khalid Razvi, PhD; *TheThe Poetry Blog Spotlight Feature*; *TheThe Poetry Blog's Infoxicated Corner*; *The NonBinary Review's Arabian Nights Issue*; *Dreamspinning*, an anthology, published by Zoetic Press; *Best Independent American Poetry 2015*, published by Goss183. The poems featured include: Eve, Eve, and Adam...Nowhere; Abida; Leonid Shower Above 360 Overlook; Chaand Raat; Eid ul Fitr; Nightmare of Ritual and Release; Of Birds, Of Prey; The Consequences of the Bedtime Story; Double Edge of Scimitar; Before the Wedding Party; American Flag as Pardah; Holy Land; Chrysopoeia: The Transmutation of An Element into Gold is the Gilding on the Screen; What the Shadow Said Before the Simurgh; Anthem for Those Ancestors; Dream with Pomegranate and Horizon of Pain; Lovesick Wanderer, O Dervish of the Restless Heart; Chalked Circles and Circumferences of Breath; Beside the Muezzin's Call and the Harem's Veil: the Ordinary Adam, this Eve. I'd like to thank the Virginia C Middleton Fellowship, the Fania Kruger Fellowship, and the James A Michener Fellowship for supporting my work. I'd also like the express my gratitude for the love, friendship, community, support, encouragement, and inspiration that so many people in my life have given me, including: my parents Tahir & Abida Syed Razvi, Shehla Razvi and Babak Mobasheri, Suemyra Razvi and Mustafa Syed, Musa, Iliyah, Zacharaiah, Mubeen, Mahir, Dr. Aziz Syed, Fox Frazier Foley, Jilly Dreadful, Mary Field, Cody Todd, Neil Aitken, Josie Sigler, J Barager, Larbi Gallagher, Suraj Shankar, Jess Piazza Kelli Anne Noftle, Amaranth Borsuk, Genevieve Kaplan, Alexis Lothian, Katy Karlin, Yetta Howard, Janalynn Bliss, Mark Marino, Matthew Siegel, Lee Ann Gallaway, Aeryck Eagle, Cody Hage, Farid Matuk, Carrie Fountain, Anna Rosen Guercio, Tim Wong, Diana Artrian, Diana Lopez, AJ Ortega, Nikki Hutchinson Davis, Dianne Gault, Charles Alexander, Cynthia Miller, Patricia Smith, Kyle Schlesinger, Margaret Rhee, Leah Maines, Christen Kincaid, Percival Everett, TC Boyle, Mark Irwin, Dana Johnson, Aimee Bender, Eamonn Wall, Fidel Fajardo Acosta, Tom Whitbread, Judith Kroll, Naomi Shihab Nye, Khaled Mattawa, Kim Herzinger, Dagoberto Gilb, Melissa Studdard, Kimiko Hahn, Roger Sedarat, Cole Swensen, David St. John, Carol Muske Dukes, Susan McCabe, Moshe Lazar, Paul Alkon, Jeffrey DiLeo, Lauren A. Pirosko, and so many more that I haven't been able to name here from among my family and friends and community. This collection honors American Muslims and others across the world, the sacrifices we make for freedom, and the hopes that we all carry for a humanity marked by peace, prosperity, and equality.

Publisher: Leah Maines
Editor: Christen Kincaid
Cover Art: Virginia Frances Sterret
Author Photo: Saba Syed Razvi
Cover Design: Elizabeth Maines

Printed in the USA on acid-free paper.
Order online: www.finishinglinepress.com
       also available on amazon.com

Author inquiries and mail orders:
Finishing Line Press
P. O. Box 1626
Georgetown, Kentucky 40324
U. S. A.

# Table of Contents

Eve, Eve, and Adam…Nowhere ..................................................................1
Girl Friend: *Saheli* ....................................................................................2
*Abida* ..........................................................................................................3
Leonid Shower Above 360 Overlook .......................................................4
*Chaand Raat: Eid ul Fitr* ..........................................................................5
The Truth Inside Postcards ........................................................................6
Nightmare of Ritual and Release ..............................................................7
Of Birds, Of Prey .........................................................................................9
Tutankhamon's Nurse ..............................................................................11
The Consequences of the Bedtime Story ..............................................12
Double Edge of Scimitar .........................................................................13
Before the Wedding Party .......................................................................14
*Habibi*: Beloved .......................................................................................15
Lupercalia ..................................................................................................16
*Keyrkadeh* ................................................................................................17
Cairo Palace Café—Houston, TX ..........................................................18
American Flag as *Pardah* .......................................................................19
Holy Land ..................................................................................................20
Port Lavaca, TX ........................................................................................21
*Chrysopoeia & Isagoge:*
    1. The Clockwork's Uncertainty Is the Shadow of the
       Unlettered Land ...........................................................................22
    2. Palimpsest of an Entry for the Book of Ingenious
       Devices ...........................................................................................24
    3. Palimpsest of Technical Drawings from the Book of
       Knowledge of Ingenious Mechanical Devices: Peacock-
       Flame, Monk-Child, Song of Fountain and Light ....................25
    4. To read by life's light is knowing, but to read the ruins
       by the smoke of watchful fires requires neither nation
       nor faith .........................................................................................26
    5. *Chrysopoeia*: The Transmutation of Any Element into
       Gold Is the Gilding on the Screen ..............................................27
The Devil of the Waning of the Ways Knows a Thing About
    Promises ..............................................................................................28
What the Shadow Said Before the *Simurgh* .........................................29
*Dervish of the Restless Heart:*
    1. Anthem for Those Ancestors ...................................................30
    2. Dream with Pomegranate and Horizon of Pain ...................32
    3. Lovesick Wanderer, O Dervish of the Restless Heart ..........33
    4. Chalked Circles and Circumferences of Breath ...................34
Beside the Muezzin's Call and the Harem's Veil: the Ordinary
    Adam, this Eve ...................................................................................36

**Eve, Eve and Adam...Nowhere**

In parts of the Mediterranean, it was not an apple
that Eve plucked from a high branch, but a fig.
In others, they say pomegranate—who
defines the size of desire, the shapes of lust?

A rush of skins on skin: plucking this fruit
is leaving herself on the vines.

It is heated work to harvest figs; I spent today weaving
through three trees;
branches newly nudged aside for honey-yellow bulbs
snap back into old places, unfurling, slap at my face.

The brightest ones soften—
already too fermented to eat.

Beneath the widest, peach-skinned grey-green leaves,
the ripest curves of bulbs shift into sight:
firm enough to grasp, pink
blush spreading from their tips, outward, into maroon.

You must twist them slowly free of their branches
until they loosen,
spilling beads of sticky, white milk
from their broken stems.

These are the ones worth rummaging for
through high, thickening branches, spiraling upward.

I brought in a basketful, rinsing off the sticky resin
in icewater
and lifting them by the handful back into dry towel.

Keep them too close and they sour quickly, unbreathing.
No pear could ever come this close to an offering.

## Girl Friend: *Saheli*

Your *dupattah* is trailing behind you, in
in the breeze like a ribbon that has wound
up and spun you, pulling your scarf—
ribboned like a snake or a bird, green
and parroting the wind. And now you
are gathering your long tunic, *khameez*
to cover your modesty just so, the way
of Waterhouse's Boreas or shying Eve—
just one of my sighs has caught there,
too, in the hem of your lap.

Oh, I can catch the wind

in my skirts

like apples?

A breath,
strong enough to fill

all of my lap…

In Urdu, the wind is called
*Hava*, which is also how
you say Eve.

## Abida

She sits in the dawn silence—
house pulsing with dreams
& *muezzin* echoes of a faith
deeper than sleep—
fingers holding prayer beads,

counting each worry
& pushing it away
with a small *tick*
to clash into the others
on the strand of her *tasbeeh*.

Her prayer rug secure beneath her—
threadbare reds & blues
where knees & forehead have
ground faith deep
into *terra firma*.

A flame to burn down heaven,
& a sea to quench hell
& like Rabia
she sits before God,
offers her love for itself alone.

Later, there will be coffee, tea,
to be made,
sugar spoons & aspartame,
too many kinds of cracked
& cooking eggs, a rush of hands.

The sound of crumpling paper
sacks, screen doors slamming
against *Thanks*,
echoed in the scattered, unrinsed
mugs & shells.

And every 4am,
her threadbare rectangle like solid stone
waits, the beads ticking
a loop of steady gratitude.
Everywhere—peace.

## Leonid Shower Above 360 Overlook

       i.
Crisp November hours. Still.
And the stone beneath my back is softer than sea
or river reflecting beneath.

Wide before me stretch mist and textured sky.
Quick bursts of sudden glitter, thrust
swift through cloud cover.

Night breeze thrumming a stiff chorus of leaf
sounds, muffled whispers in hidden faces.
And rock cradles arm cradles head.

Dark pulls down my eyelids, full
of the blush of the gloaming. Then silver
streams like marionette strings to keep me watching.

       ii.
The *Sijjin* weighs heavy on my low left side
and I grip my right fist, to balance deed with desire.

*The shades of night are slipping*
*over your fingertips,*
          velveteen like the green whispers beside me.

No moon sickle sweet to threaten my high neck in the dark
of sky, but the crescents of nails digging into my palm will
scar like stone under ice water.

*Are you counting how many per moment*
*little slips of falling fire?*
          demons sent flailing from heaven
  with broken bits of gossip.

I measure the silent angle, the trajectory of stone.

It is only me here:

cliff face, an empty plateau holding
my splayed fingers behind me,
my sprawling legs before me,
and my knees locked flat.

Doll on a bookshelf, glassy eyes dreaming
          of something more real than faith,
  watching the fall of heavens beneath her feet.

**Chand Raat:** *Eid ul Fitr*

Greensweet
henna in sugar-oil and eucalyptus,
I trace
in hair-thin coils,
along my upturned paling palms.

Beneath this
bouquet of temporary futures,
twined with blossoms opening in my night,
your own
wishes—palmlined map
to the walls of the city inside my breath.
These worldly wishes in red, drying lines—
only complements.

I go tonight,
not to the bridal chamber of a man,
but to the thinnest crescent of a moon.
Hear these, my bangles, Beloved.
Here, these my knees—cracking—
on which I kneel towards
the Easterly.

I have left it behind, Beloved.

The laughter of carnival
in the distance,
a bright-lit bazaar,
shop-keepers selling sandalwood or myrrh,
rock-sugar candy,
beads on which to count Your name.

It is enough
for me—
these knuckles: an abacus under thin skin,
a carpet of green grass blades,
the nightbirds in the wind—
and in the wind,
tendrils of my hair lifting off my nape.

Light rising from resting in contours everywhere.

## The Truth Inside Postcards

I call her and I give her the hours of dawn to translate,
thin beams
of daylight warming the silent air in my apartment.

She masks her eyes with glasses, furrowed brows,
bustles to her bookshelf,
laying out before her lap an assortment of bound pages:
thin, too frail to carry,
fat with curling pages, scrolls like brittle
papyrus, in English, Urdu, Arabic,
and she says *Inshallah, he will make it something good;*
*wait, wait…*
*here, talk to your father while I look.*

My mother, patient oracle, tells me cryptic answers
that only my heavy heart can understand, and only
in these morning-yellow moments,
before the heavy tides of night lose the messages
hatching from swan eggs into peacock feather,
under a hurricane sky, when everything is
anticipation—*leave him if he hurts you so; you are losing*
*faith like the tide; there will always be words to come;*
*someday, you will shine like the inside of moon.*

My sisters, too, still in pajamas and last night's makeup,
will join her for tea at the table
ask her to mend their kaleidoscopic midnights into meaning
while my father fries eggs, silently listening.

Miles of telephone wire bind the dreaming—
    even as far as Omaha, gray Ohio,
    the wet-sandy monsoons in Madras—
a simple board & chain swing under a thorny, bitter-berried tree—
    the dusty, flame-colored markets of Hyderabad,
    or the dry, flat horizons of Texas—
and leave my tea leaves to settle
a blurry word in my cup, a word—so much like *home*.

## Nightmare of Ritual and Release

In the language of our shared heritage, the number three,
the number three,
the number three bears a ritual significance.

In the language of our shared heritage,
the gates of paradise rest at the feet of the mother,
the woman who bears us, who bears…all of us, and all besides.

Because, you say, the world of the creator belongs to those who believe.
Because you always believed that for those who believed in their God,
the letting go of this life is a release.

In the language of our shared heritage,
death is only a return to the embrace of the creator, womb of the eternal
 mother,
for those who are steadfast in faith and belief.

But, for those who hesitate, pacing back and forth, back and forth, back
 and—
is it forth if you refuse to go forward, if you live in the past like it never
 changed?—

forth? The door opens and closes on reality and I walk
into the room and out of the room and avoid the third time.

In the language of our shared heritage, the number three means consent,
means a certain acknowledgment,

means  I cannot bite my tongue again to taste the red of our shared
 heritage
to avoid walking into a room bearing you but not you.

As I think of you, I think of you, thinking of your own mother.
As I think of you, I think of your own grief.
As I think of you, I cannot bear to walk into that room and bear the
 weight of my grief.

It is the ritual washing of the body that I remember. You taught me this,
myself, my sister, my other sister, three. You taught me this. And without
 you, I have lost them, too.
The red of my bitten lip, the cells that will tell me what came before what

will come again.

The mother, the maiden, the crone.
The lover, the liver, the stone.
The mother, my mother, my own.

I raise your hand, chant a prayer, chant a prayer, right first, rinse the water
    thrice over each.
Your gold bracelets not chiming like bells, your fingers broad like mine,
    your nails, strong like mine,
you said I had your hands; so, I think of your hands washing mine.

I raise your left hand thrice beneath the water, watch the water fall
    downward
through the drain in the floor, watch the water slip down the drain, as
    when you
bathed the body of your own mother, that water took with it the band of
    your wedding ring.

I wash your face, face like my own face, face that I cannot face
Because as long as I have wanted you to understand my voice or my own
    words,
I cannot see you face me, now, voice the words, now, that I would hear,
    now.

Before I wrap your body in a sheet,
before I let you go from me,
before I recognize what you say that death for the beloved of God is a
    relief,

I wash your arms. I wash your feet. First the right three times, then the
    left three times,
With you my heritage ends, with me, your lineage ends; such time until
    we meet again.
Paradise lies under the feet of the mother, Paradise rests beneath the feet
    of the mother.

**Of Birds, Of Prey**

If you were eight years old, awake
early enough in the morning for the treat of a walk
with your older brothers, worldwise and unweary yet,
you might feel big in your trousers,
chappals, big enough to see the wonders of the sky.

If you were eight years old then, and roaring,
like lions, like tigers, two planes emerged
from the poles of the horizon, erupting
into a dogfight over your own veranda,
you might think it was a game. Such a show of. Until
the horror on your brothers' faces showed otherwise.

And if you were eight years old still,
heart racing in the center of a circle
of siblings, your father and same brothers armed
heavier than the servants, you might have stayed
up all night, tense as a violin string
because the communists were coming over the fields,
because your father was appointed
by the British and India discovered an urge for freedom.

And what if you were still eight, traveling in a coal car,
a formation of aeroplanes like geese flying overhead?
Covered with soot and holding breath, you might begin
to understand how the world bears cruelty in the horizon's arms—
it's certainty in the metal birds
that freedom for Hyderabad had been lost. At any moment
the train could screech to a halt, armed men checking
each boxcar.

If you were eight years old, the war raging all around you and
only just over the horizon, you would not feel the way forward
was a promise. You would know better
than to resort to the contentious names for things, the names
everyone wants to choose—an apple is the fruit that made you fall
in love with the world, a cloud of smoke is a reminder of hearth
and home, needing the wanderer's safe return. A man is nothing
but a body made of clay, made of longing and fear, in need of a name.

If you were eight years old when fighter planes roared

beyond your head, you would wonder at the way fire had gone
from hearth to heart of artillery, and you might wonder what words
and what beyond words keeps safe the questioning glance, and you
would remember that beyond the gates of your door was nothing
sure as death. Atmosphere carrying the threat of ambush:
not every dancer is a dervish;
what is the difference between a dogfight and a drone?

At seventy-eight, you would have never forgotten the taste of fear, coal
in your lungs, silence. Your world-curious, word-wise daughters—never
safe. How can you explain it to them, the danger of a voice, a perfect sky,
how quickly a stroll can pull you under the rain
of revolution? Any sky can burst in a moment. Any man—a hunter,
turning weak before a tiger.

## Tutankhamon's Nurse

How easy—to unbury
the dead,
as if corpses might speak
over the din of epoch.
> *What can we do with so much*
> *displaced sand?*

At Saqqara, past mounds
of cat mummies—an
alabaster jar
of organs: a sign
that the labyrinthine tombs
waited so many suns
under sand
to give us a story—
in the heart, Maya.
You pull husks of men out
of their waiting for rebirth,
excavate
subterranean cities, and
they plunder tombs
for black market gold,
sacrifice hand-
lain walls for the same.
Would you break the bricks
of the living to honor
your footsteps the spirit
of the dead?
> *Make the tallest dunes,*
> *abandon them to sunburnt wind!*

The nature of sand varies. Soft
as sun-ashes where we tread, it is
cold, dark, wet above the mummies.
We create no *shartis*,
vessels to testify our deeds,
no graven deities to protect us.

Because our deaths are solitary.
We move
the tongues of sand
until they grant us tales
of an opulence
that we could not even want.

## The Consequences of the Bedtime Story

It was a skeleton who robbed its East
   of silks to thread its bones in films
      of scented oils and colored stones to fill
         the sockets of its eyes and lips.
In the desert, it found blood beneath
   the unforgiving, shifting sands,
      diamond blood, the clotting coal—
         an amniotic song.
It was a shadow of a deathly king
   who held his scepter high. Bone-made,
      this staff he held—beside his halo dry—
         over men who could not buy these tides.
It was not a man of flesh or sin who could be held
   against the mercies of the sun,
      or to the justice of the crows to pluck
         irises, one and one—left for guilt
      or right for clean—or heart for scales to judge.
Brief frame of bones, shadow lengthened artillery-sharp,
   it sought a tongue of coins
      to fill its grasp, to bribe the ferry-man,
         to weight the story still held close but slipping
            through a cage-empty chest, a wrong red hand.

## Double Edge of Scimitar

Trim your beard
a little bit shorter this time,
*haaji*, so your wife doesn't
smell the other woman,
still young enough to
water like a peach,
still innocent enough to think
your attentions
will lead her ascent to heavens
beyond your *hafiz* flesh.
And don't forget to shower
before you step
onto the newly-swept floor,
past the table laid out
with your wife's delicate
touch spread banquet-wide
and festive
because she knows it
isn't her you're gracing these nights,
you quick as the binding needle,
swift as the unbinding knife,
her unstitched
warmth too familiar and still
not tight enough to hold
away the clenching of a fist.
Remember, she'll lie
still as a floorboard, for you,
all the dusty creaks you expect,
but, no, don't
stay long or she will notice
other splinters, hardened
in your tauter muscles.
Better to leave her
unrewarded, contemplating her errors,
the barren hollow inside the waist,
how much more compliant she should be.

### Before The Wedding Party

Textured velvet *ghararra*, skirt heavy and veil heavier,
filled crimson with gold and the intricacies of needled

fingers into patterns that catch and dispel the light
into so many glares. It is easy to sit still, head

down under a *ghoongat* veil in modest pose, when secrets
hang like sharp garlands, stone-laden at the neck,

red lips frowning at once willful knees now folded like hands
too folded on them. It befits a bride to wring her nervous

fingers, let go a show of scalding tears in anticipation.

But there's a fine unseen line, slit-skin slender, dividing
modesty from shame. Old customs die too

                                          slowly, survive the young
opening angles of hips and hands, to face the limbs' deceits.

What answer then when with *henna*-ed hands so much red
undress sheds like a chameleon's skill to the ground? When

the body pales the way of sheets on which there is nothing
but white like the silent and frightened flag of surrender.

Close of ceremony nearing, and in the mirror coy between
them, jasmine-garlanded reflections leave no space

for a slip of tongue or blade, or indecent bite to split
the blanched expanse

of dread.                        Bloodlust spent without blood,

blankness to explain.

*Habibi*: **Beloved**

This, the *zaghreet* call in the dervish whirl
of your waist, is a shudder in the sheen of your

*Dance!*, now, like the serpent skinned
behind your eyes knew not how to fade.

                                                          My own

eyes drinking your wavering hips. The braid
of tambourine uncoiling as you speak,

tastes like smoke, like coffee. It hangs
in my hair after you have forgotten

the scythe of crescent hanging in the slick
edge of black, bladed night.

                                      In you, I could

build houses, live like earthen men—made
of half spirit and half sand. Under the red

embers of coal, your lips, the swell of burning
and of exhaled smoke—Are you, behind it, only

a mirage spilling in a peasant's skirt
to appease a crowd, high waving fingers only

the cadence of rising voices, the hollow beat
of drum matching your cruel, quick feet?

                                                  Nothing

but a colored swirl of light and smoke, leaved tea.

## Lupercalia

Teeth and tawn and taut and tone.
        Fiery face ringed round with bone
Wash the sound of ripping thigh
        From the spreading-open sly

Of every dusk's descent toward
        Hunger. A heady lusty
Scent that breathes me deeper in
        The tall pines against nightskin.

Give me the gristle of the girl
        The lush of her sweet curls
As they stick against lapping
        Tongue and tulip colored sting,

As they fade from taste into the face
Of girl white moon and crimson lace.

### Keyrkadeh

There, in a village outside Cairo—
its name I have forgotten, beginning
with a sound like
No…

Hibiscus blossoms, plump
& bright as flame wait to be plucked,
drying dark as clots of blood
in the sun.

*If you have never drunk their tea, red
as your open veins, tart
enough to pucker your lips unwillingly,
sweetened*

*with the honey of wildflowers,
you have never known
the meaning of seduction*, he had said—
So many kinds of crimson

falling into tastes, never
really left behind.
Watch it brew witches brew in you, water
thickening from nothing. The color

moves so slow. How long it takes to cool;
it will, always the first time, burn your tongue.

### Cairo Palace Café—Houston, TX

Walking into a well-lit hookah bar after midnight, we didn't
expect a half-empty table full of family-friends—

It was supposed to be a night for siblings, for catching up
with sisters for *I'm finally wearing lipstick again.*

In dragon-breathing moments, surrounded by exhaled apple,
grape, strawberry flavored tobacco,

it is easy to slip into the oldest shoes, into voices spoken
against the bubbling of *arghileh*, into stormwhile stories.

It is easy to pass these violet hours here, among the nameless
faces with the same color skin, almost-familiar accents.

So we sit here, wrapped up in smoking rows of speaking,
chess moves and carom, belly dancers, *keyrkadeh* and mint tea.

In the center of an unexpected gathering, it feels not unlike
huddling together in a long-ago windowless room

instead of evacuating, while Hurricane Alicia's screeching
winds brought a fence down on our strawberry patches,

gifted our front lawn with an additional rooftop. Our parents'
stories of older generations fell then in the same accents

around us, songs turned to rain so hard it echoes still
in water bubbles, the sky dissipating like smoke.

## American Flag as *Pardah*

Baghdad, of its magic carpets, lost
one thread and another—like a crumpling row
of soldiers—in turn, the rectangles folding
back over themselves, and the tasseled fringes
of sky and soil met, across the horizon.

A hem was pulled from the vertical center—
one row of stitching, square knots
of windows and curtains—and another
above, higher, above, unraveling
into the collapsing spine of the building,
sides falling into the center, into a plume
like an ash flower, an asphodel—
the ghost of bodied breath swelling
under a snapping sky.

In TX, I folded my *jah-e-namaz*, fringe to fringe,
to place my peace on an American shelf
beside the TV screen
on which the whistles of bursting rocket lulled
unfinished screams—
until I stopped folding
my scarf into smaller angles in my frozen hands—
my scarf on my hands, under my eyes opening,
fell open unfolding—openmouthed, unsilenced.

## Holy Land

Inside every field of sunflowers, one
*can* find a field of suns—and so
every
soldier fights for something noble.
But
in each free movement by a one,
is the slavery of another. One
head held high only
because another is bowed
to give it light—a shadow anchors
every stem.
                        Nothing can exist
except in absolutes.

Every east must be another's west.

The lines we carve on maps, mortal
          as skin.
Each split hemisphere will open
like a sliced sun.
One half falling,
held half dripping
down the grasping hand.
                        Nothing
left to balance the scale.
                        Instead,
we make fences over bones;
their gardens mark the weight of air.

## Port Lavaca, Texas

My sister and I walk along the curving pier.
Beside us, through slate-grey cloud cover
fat bands of sun fall down to flooded grass
where the waves ripple like melted silver.
We are looking for marsh birds.
But there are no great egrets stretching their long rope necks,
no pelicans filling cupped beaks with fish—
except in bold black strokes on the signs.
There are only laughing gulls
gathering in formation
like fleets of aeroplanes or small winged soldiers,
behind us.
And a series of black skimmers, lining the guardrail
beside us
that take flight one by one as we pass.
A silent fanfare of feather and beak announces our turn
of the curve to the gazebo.
Totems of summer flings carved into splintered benches, in fading
marker, M ❤ Q 4-ever, Jenni + Matt = luv, palimpsest others.
We speak of our lost loves like birds, hastening into cloudless sky;
the planks full of broken pairs
and so we empty our pockets of perfect seashells in offering:
maybe one set of carved letters will remain undefeated.
Nothing through the rows of telescopes but wave and grass,
our magnified friends splashing waves farther down the shore.
Retreating, we toss bits of Oreo and the fleet of aeroplane gulls lifts
simultaneously, some swooping to catch chocolate in orange beaks,
the rest poised mid-air and waiting.
Past the edge of pier, the waves crash at our ankles,
at a jellyfish on sea foam, caught
at the barrier between tide and dry shore.
But on the walk back, when the tide rises high,
having carried our sandals into the current, leaving us
to watch after them,
a sudden red heron hunches over, carries off its prey in sharp beak.
We stand gazing after the heron,
sandals forgotten though the sand cakes between our wet toes.
It is like this, love—predatory and perched,
ready to take flight without warning.

## Chrysopoeia & Isagoge

1.
### The Clockwork's Uncertainty Is the Shadow of the Unlettered Land

> (after Ahmed, and all the innocent clocks in Irving, TX causing fear in the hearts of the heartless)

> "The Smattering I have of the philosopher's stone (which is something more than the perfect exaltation of gold) hath taught me a great deale of Divinity." —Thomas Browne, Religio Medici, Part 1:38.

                        Said the bigot to the boy, mouth bigger with
                        guns than grammar:

You are not a man but
child of a man, but something
common, core and creature—
a homunculus.

                        Your ticking and clicking
                        and perpetually burning
                        cannot be as simple as
                        a lamp or a clock,
                        but both are bright as a burst

explosive, a malleable
glass can make
a malleable man, a trans-
mutation of the unprecious
dead, a lapis loon, a mood.

                        You are not a machine you, child
                        maker of making, of
                        the mechanical, of the rosary
                        that is not a rose garden
                        but a word you see and will not read
                        along with elemental fifths,
                        of *al iksir,* stone of red sulfur and you
                        glow like a hot coal, not a child
                        whose name I will consent to know.

Your face is too proud, too, not ingenious,
your mechanical device is just a legendary
danger, the sand man is a sand monster
turning the horizon into glass and you

                                                        are not what I think should be free.

2.
**Palimpsest of an Entry for the Book of Ingenious Devices**

The brothers of the house of wisdom built
    a book. A thousand and one less one by ten
and the brothers of the house of wisdom built
    devices and a page on a page on how to use them.
The brothers of the house of wisdom built
    a hero or a *philo-* or a system of control.
The brothers of the house of wisdom built
    a pneumatic valve. // What use would you have
for a pneumatic valve, or // engineering among
    the eighth century sands? But in the works of
the hand of the once-Vitruvian Man is
    the power that doesn't need reason to
        *reason.*
The brothers of the house of wisdom built
    a trick of the mind, a vessel, moving water, out of time,
a fountain in a flower of tin, feathers, a shape shifter
    in the wind, a musical box with a flute and a claw,
        a gas mask for covering the face.
The brothers of the house of wisdom built
    a trick of the mind and wonder. // What wonder
can we find in a sand and cattled land beside
    frontiers and borders, where the house carries
the memory of the ranks of color, unmoored, unmoved with
    the movement of time?//
The brothers of the house of wisdom built
    // what I will call nothing but a book of tricks, and
you are not the color of wisdom I will recognize//
The brothers of the house of wisdom built a book
    by which you made a gauge to give us time and wonder,
but // I will not read by it, or give your light any other word than
    dark to be given back to darkness.//
The brothers of the house of wisdom built a book; in the book:
devices to dazzle the movement of wit and time, water, shadow, fire.

## 3.
**Palimpsest of Technical Drawings from the Book of Knowledge of Ingenious Mechanical Devices: Peacock-Flame, Monk-Child, Song of Fountain and Light.**

The sacred letter is the song of any scribe, sound and sense bound in the simplest strokes, graceful turn and punishing constraint but the sense and the sensing bound at once. The sacred stone is a shape, a displacing clay, a geometry of material that shadows the light. The shifting of the numbers of the stone and tree, the rhizome's offering to algae and ant, and the slivers of those shapes make up the faces of edifices of the sacred, where may be seated the songs of the pious, bearing the lettered lingering of the mewling, guttural wish of the pit of navel and the curve of the nape of the neck, curving skyward. The shape, repeating is a structure. The structure of bone is a cathedral, a temple, a mosque, a library, a rosary on which to count the many sins of the sacred and the unsacred and the scared are simpler to reach by song. And if the song is kept in keyed tin, in fountains opening at the mooring of the peacock's ominous throaty warble, a portent to slip open a pocket or a portal to the rivers of the garden, like the rivers extinguishing a small flame born by a tin monk bearing in his lap a child, lifting a cup to the shore of tin bridged on the other side. The letter letters the world, the world letters the sound, the sound letters the name, and the name is the song of being and light. And what of the words curling like henna on the body, inklovely tattoos on the body's walls, and the body is the building of a sacred space now lettered with words that unsing the spoilt song of a screen-built homeland or the ruins of a hand-bricked wall, walling the gardener from gardens of orange and olive grove, from the rivers in sunny land. Where does the land dip open and fold? Where is the tongue's taste for petal and leaf? Where will the mountain's path lead? And to write those many names with light, hues of neon and electricity, ephemeral as breath, is to say that the word is a world of words, worldlied and world-weary and wearing the sacred songs, the stroke of the scribe there beyond the world of the unread, velvet and ripe for the asking and the eating and the taking of this breath—a voice commands you to look at the letters of your dreams and read…

4.
**To read by life's light is knowing, but to read the ruins by the smoke of watchful fires requires neither nation nor faith.**

> *"One is the Serpent which has its poison according to two compositions, and One is All and through it is All, and by it is All, and if you have not All, All is Nothing."* —From the Chrysopoeia of Cleopatra.

**You say** you know the words, **but if** the Angel Gabriel came to **you** and said, "Read!", could you? What mark upon your heart is there to **decipher** if not made by the maker of **your heart, burned into a flame** you spill upon the other? **Your black flag** is no brotherhood. **Your wrath** is not worthy of the vessels or the vestments **you fill** inside **your desire** for humiliation. What is **the word you know,** if **it means nothing but** razing to wraith what wordlessly offends you, **what signs make a shap**e you can see as **something**? The sign stands for a thing seen. The thing seen for **what is known**. What you know is not the same all all-knowing and what signs **may point** to one land in one time point **to ruins** in **another**. What is the **word you seek**, call out in the dark of **battle, weep** into your waiting, **leave** to linger in **the space between the taking of the stars and the taker? Your darkness is not** a sign of **something other than your refusal** to read the mark that the maker did not make, your masked face, **your nothing** masked with the black of night on which you find **an empty word, nothing** at all **like surrender** to the sign of all things.

O, you who heed the **glory-hued, growing like** the weeds among your poppies, **what** are the colors that **you bleed**? When you sleep, do you dream you are nothing like **the draught of poppy,** not your jeans or your tobacco fields, not your league of long-lineaged assassins from the caricatured pages, provoking all **the shades of blood and bile** and grey, **not your prism** spectrum collapsed beneath **crusade from** all **hue to** no **hue**? Your palms **dyed the hue of demons** falling from the stars? **Marked**, like the first brother and the first kill. Every brother, every kill. **And, so,** not every land with lines around it is a landed law, a state of one thing. And, so, not every line is made **in oil and sand and smoke and fear. And** not every stroke of **pen** must be **rendered by fire and blade,** by a hastening shame. **The serpent seeks** only **the** circled **taste of itself**, its unweighted scales in spills of iridescence, **its teeth** taking in **its tail.**

5.
**_Chrysopoeia_: The Transmutation of Any Element into Gold Is the Gilding on the Screen**

Rumplestiltzkin taught the maiden to spin the straw into gold. She sat in a tower made of ivory.
> The transmutation of a thing into another thing, wherein the
> thing is substrate and another thing is the precipitate
> of a philosophy made of life-clay and breath, is
> something of a work of greatness, greatening the grating hours
> of harsh day as its sun slips into illumination and silvery sheen.

> > Every night is a howl of wolves,
> > weres wearing a sound that stops
> > the unturning humors cold.

She spun the straw, but she did not spin the straw. Her shadow spun the straw and so she spun the straw.

> It is the leaden that is led by an anger, reactive and reactionary, an
> alembic among the people, led into a leading energy in service of
> a wizening. The crude cut of the desire is the clarity, the clear-
> eyed cleaving of a word that means another word for something
> of a complication beyond complicity.

> > Hurt hands and hearts, are unclear
> > about clarity beyond a grievance
> > of blood and bone and blight.

Man saw a shadow where she was, spinning, and in the dawn the straw had been replaced by gold.

> But, seeing what is sought is just a seeing in the darkening light, a
> seeing that says and that says all lamps are lit, and the light on the
> other shadow is a perpetual blaze, a burning beyond the properties
> of element.

> > Fire demands fire, demands fire,
> > demands something to turn into
> > the certainty of ash or glimmer.

And, so. She spun. Straw. Into gold.

## The Devil of the Waning of the Ways Knows a Thing About Promises

This
        all this that
you
        want and wanted more than
desire
        wound through you, you can halve by
half
        the having—
        of your faith in faith in shadows
Your life
        your bite of supple flesh,
sweet
        with dripping enough to soak
        those brittle bones, drying
        from the marrow
woven
        in their weaving
for the price of your doubt in

what

You can
        *not* become brittleborn
        like a clay blanching
        in the vessel soaking in all of
this
        sun and sky.
You do not have
        to fall into ash
Give me the given, the gotten, the green
and all

this
        is
sand
        in your palms.

## What the Shadow Said Before the *Simurgh*

Circle of air, circle of salt, you do not know my name.
Circle of sand, filling with the darkness
and the wet strings of rot, you
bind me, you
contain me, you
remind me that
this song is my wood and my grove,
my compass, my snow
split with the maw of your tongue's lust,
red like this is a whisper in the darkness
you hold fevered at bay, that these
the bonds we make in shadow and blood
bring power and the song of searing
so surrendering apart because
every man
would bow his head before the kiss of Sekhmet,
its toothy sound, an openness, a gristle
like the mudfilled milky vessel
of man in pain, kneeling. Circle of clay,
it calls you just there, beyond, it
opens a door, moonwhite and angry,
moonspilt and seeking for glassy eyes,
fishwide,
feathers and lenses, lore for the market, lyre
for the magician long forgotten in
your shadow, in the blood clotting in your bones,
for the one you woke
with your pen.
I am unwritten in the breeze.
Do not call me forth.
Write your love in saffron, in oil, in the hues
of sacrifice and grief, circle your sounds
in the glyph of shadow
in blazing light; hear me, and do not answer my call.

*Dervish of the Restless Heart*

1.
**Anthem for those Ancestors**

>   *(after the Kundiman & Kaya Press AWP Seattle Bruce Lee Party)*

I don't have, for you, a Bruce Lee poem.

I don't have a poem about an elephant speaking
>   in the voice of Ganesh.

I don't have the verse that versus the fundamentalist
>   impulse to blow shit up that you don't like.

I don't have one foot in one land or one in another.

I don't know the name for myself that isn't diaspora.

I don't fit enough into one tongue or another,

>   but I miss the tongue of that cowboy coming
>   back home in a big truck,
>   still smelling of fracking and the fuel fields.

I don't have, for you, a poem on the occasion of the
>   owning of the race of the racists.

I don't have a voice stifled for you beneath some unchosen veil.

I don't have, for you, words that speak your language.

I don't have, for you, words that say "approval"—not
>   from home, nor from home away from home, either.

I don't have, for you a poem, about the nation of my
>   name,

>   -------- just the sinewy sibilance of my fingers,
>   scratching out sighs on a page,

>   while I think of that good ole once upon a cowboy
>   saying "I don't really read such books that often",

all the while reading stories on my skin, his fingers writing
silence
        on my sunbrowned sin, and

my thoughts reaching out to hold his bearded face,
pull his hips close to mine so that I am filled with a

forgetfulness
              of words that I cannot name, or
unlearn how to say.

Those places he has been, I have not; he has seen
the sands that gave me my name,
        *Kan yama kan, Qaf* and beyond.

I do not have for you a poem about the nomad in my blood
    that knows these sandsongs that I cannot, do not
    know how, to say—

Oh, tie-ers of knots, untie my tongue, unknot what
I do not have, for you, a poem about.

2.
## American :: Dream, with Pomegranate and Horizon

> *(On the occasion of the departure of forces, US and NATO, after twelve years of war in Afghanistan)*

In the water of the scrying bowl, strings of silver curl into the letters of some foreign alphabet, letters formed of smoke and fog, of sand and kohl, palimpsests, of fire, fireless flame, firefly shame, starlight and otherworldly breath, pluming in the cold of desertscapes. // I dream you, fatigued, in fatigues, flesh charred, but in tact, singed and covered in soot, but alert and alive, more stunned than bled, your eyes, smiling—luminous, bright and blue as a drone-ready sky. // I dream you gathering seeds in the land of pomegranates, scattering them along the mountainsides, the sandy dunes, the horizon like a lion's mane curling as the beast startles into some readied stance. // And, as I miss your fingers tracing the language of my lost tongue along my skin, the words I do not know, bursting into lush green life inside me, fire and flame and flower petals the color of spring. // I dream you safe and crossing currents of air and smoke toward an unsettled home, a waiting home, your hand scattering those gathered seeds with an open hand. And, when is April like a bride in Spring, the cypresses scenting the breeze? // I dream that they sprout flesh along barren terrain left behind, hearts, beating fruit, budding with fear and with frustration, with the anticipation of a coming storm.

3.
**Lovesick Wanderer, O Dervish of the Restless Heart**

Whirling like the morning's salt-scented breeze, over soft dunes until
  the sandstorm
tumult in me spins out unembraced across the whole of the horizon

Whirling like the wind over stark sandy dunes until the whole of me fills
  the horizon
uplifting in maddening tumult, enraptured by the sun's face on every
  grain of time

Whirling like the rising and rising is a forever forgetting of a lightless
  descent into arid
desert embrace, sand singing the whole of me to the skeletal skein of
  horizon

## 4.
## Chalked Circles and Circumferences of Breath

> *The 14th Dalai Lama said, in a 1985 ceremony, that "Shambhala is not an ordinary country…We can only say that it is a pure land, a pure land in the human realm."*
>
> *In the mid 1300s, Ibn Battuta walked 730,000 miles on foot, more than 29 times the earth's circumference (24901.55 miles), chronicling his travels, before returning to his journey's beginning. Many surmised that he returned only after finding Shambhala.*

Go as far north as you can and find snow

Go as far south as you can and find snow

Go as far east as you can Go and it becomes west again, far back as where you began.

Find me a shelf of colored bottles, a votive for a lovèd's grave, a silent room with tables waiting for a hot cup or a clean glass.

Find me a colorless flag full of flagpoles mined from every step between, threaded, knotted as many times as steps.

I would not walk 10,000 miles, coming back to another start of ten thousand miles, x times around the world until home is home again.

Along this way, onward this way, the air reddens, purples, blues into a darkness curving all, around, a tunnel leaving only the path as far as I can expel a light, spotlight, pocket, long wail of longing for sleep.

Go as far north as you can Go and find snow

Go as far south as you can Go and find snow

Go as far east as you can Go and it becomes a star, becomes west again,

    far back as where it began.

Find me a sheaf of colored pages, a bloom for the baby's crib, a silent room with a warm cup, awaiting tables.

At a curve of miles onto miles, find me.

## Beside the Muezzin's Call and the Harem's Veil: the Ordinary Adam, this Eve.

Beyond the call of the tearful muezzin ringing from minarets and medieval days, beyond the veil of the harems' unwalled pillars, its courtyard of courtesans and curves, fountains wet with oases of longing, for the parched past mirage, the world of the unwanted Arab Spring beckons, the world past the colony and the empire, past the purpled, puckered, promise of an ancient echo of a renascence long past. Beside the bragging rights of the terrorist and the terrified, the vilified and victimized, the silence of the voiceless echoes, the call to prayer and to arms, to hearth and to home and to harbor, the *zagreet* and the wail and the worried echo, beseeching or seeking, the sound of the shudder under the warplane's war cry. Beyond this, beside this, waiting for the storm to pass lies the ordinary man, the Adam with hurts as commonplace as blue jeans, his skin as alien as some ancient blue. The ordinary woman with an ordinary womb, and the curves and cries of Eve. The old man and the thin man. The seductress and the dance of her seven veils. The borrowed promise of a people to weigh the scales of some man's fat greed. And all the blameless believers, believing in nothing but a hope beyond the word beside the man who judges what is ours and what is other. The guileless stand, preemptively judged. Not that sky, but this sky. Not that name, but this name. And every atmosphere from one horizon to another ringing with the thunderous burst of the weight of atom and atom and atom.

Saba Syed Razvi is the author of *In the Crocodile Gardens* (Agape Editions, 2016), *Limerence and Lux* (Chax Press, 2016), *Of the Divining and the Dead* (Finishing Line Press, 2012), and the forthcoming collection *heliophobia*.

Her poems have appeared in journals such as *The Offending Adam, Diner, TheTHE Poetry Blog's Infoxicated Corner, The Homestead Review, NonBinary Review, 10x3 plus, 13th Warrior Review, The Arbor Vitae Review,* and *Arsenic Lobster*, among others, as well as in anthologies such as *Voices of Resistance: Muslim Women on War Faith and Sexuality, The Loudest Voice Anthology, The Liddell Book of Poetry, Political Punch: Contemporary Poems on the Politics of Identity, The Rhysling Award Nominee Anthology, The 2015 Independent Best American Poetry* anthology, and others. Her poems have been nominated for the Best of the Net Award, the Rhysling Award, and have won a 2015 Independent Best American Poetry Award.

She is currently an Assistant Professor of English and Creative Writing at the University of Houston in Victoria, TX, where in addition to teaching, she is working on scholarly research on interfaces between science and contemporary poetry, on Sufi poetry in translation, and on writing new poems and fiction.

www.ingramcontent.com/pod-product-compliance
Lightning Source LLC
LaVergne TN
LVHW041552070426
835507LV00011B/1053